McGraw-Hill Reading

Wonders

Benchmark Assessment

McGraw Hill Education

Bothell, WA • Chicago, IL • Columbus, OH • New York, NY

www.mheonline.com/readingwonders

McGraw Hill Education

Send all inquiries to:
McGraw-Hill Education
Two Penn Plaza
New York, New York 10121

Printed in the United States of America

6 7 8 9 RHR 17 16 15 14
C

The McGraw·Hill Companies

Table of Contents

Benchmark Assessment

Benchmark Assessment is an integral part of the complete assessment program aligned with ***McGraw-Hill Reading Wonders*** and the Common Core State Standards (CCSS).

Purpose of *Benchmark Assessment*

Benchmark Assessment is designed to measure how well your children acquire the reading and language arts knowledge and skills assessed on standardized tests. The results of ***Benchmark Assessment*** serve as a summative assessment by providing a way to measure children's progress through the CCSS-aligned curriculum. The results of the assessments can be used to inform subsequent instruction, aid in making leveling and grouping decisions, and point toward areas in need of reteaching or remediation.

Focus of *Benchmark Assessment*

Benchmark Assessment focuses on key areas of English Language Arts as identified by the CCSS—comprehension of literature and informational text, vocabulary acquisition and use, phonics and word recognition, command of the conventions of the English language, and writing within the parameters of specific text types.

Administering *Benchmark Assessment*

Administer Test 1 mid-year, after instruction for Units 1-3 has been completed. Administer Test 2 at the end of the year. Make copies of the benchmark assessment for the class. You will need one copy of the Answer Key page that features the scoring table for each child taking the assessment. This table provides a place to list children's scores. The data from each benchmark assessment charts children's progress and underscores strengths and weaknesses.

When scheduling the benchmark assessment, you will need to decide whether to administer it in one or more sessions. For example, for Test 2 you may choose to give the first section in one sitting and schedule the writing prompt for another time.

After each child has a copy of the assessment, provide a version of the following directions:

If you choose to read the assessment aloud, say: *Write your name and the date on the question pages for this test.* (When children are finished, continue with the directions.) *I will read the test aloud. Follow along as I read.*

If you choose to have the children read the assessment themselves, say: *Write your name and the date on the question pages for this test.* (When children are finished, continue with the directions.) *You will read one poem and two stories and answer questions. Read the poem, the stories, and the questions carefully. Make sure to completely fill in the circle next to the correct answer.* (Add the following for Test 2.) *For the writing prompt, plan your writing in the space under the prompt and write your response on the lined page. When you have completed the test, put your pencil down and turn the pages over. You may begin now.*

Answer procedural questions during the assessment. After the class has completed the assessment, ask children to verify that their names and the date are written on the necessary pages.

Overview of *Benchmark Assessment*

Each benchmark assessment is composed of the following:

- 3 "Cold Read" selections
- 15 multiple-choice items assessing Comprehension Skills
- 5 multiple-choice items assessing High-Frequency Words (Test 1)
- 5 multiple-choice items assessing Vocabulary Strategies (Test 2)
- 4 multiple-choice items assessing Structural Analysis
- 10 multiple-choice items assessing English Language Conventions
- 6 multiple-choice items assessing Phonics
- 1 Writing Prompt (Test 2)

Reading Selections

Each benchmark assessment features three "Cold Read" selections. Selection complexity mirrors the rigor of reading materials children encounter in the classroom.

Comprehension

Comprehension items in each test assess understanding of the text by use of Comprehension Skills, Literary Elements, and Text Features.

Vocabulary

Vocabulary items in Test 2 ask children to demonstrate the ability to uncover the meanings of unknown and multiple-meaning words and phrases using Vocabulary Strategies.

Reading Foundations and Language

Each benchmark assessment also includes items that assess children's mastery of phonics and structural analysis skills; high-frequency words are assessed in Test 1. See the list above for the number of items of each type that are included in the assessments.

English Language Conventions/Grammar, Mechanics, Usage

Children demonstrate their command of the conventions of standard English by correcting existing drafts or completing cloze passages.

Writing

In Test 2, children craft a written response to a prompt that asks for an opinion. This activity gives children an opportunity to practice writing in a test situation and is consistent with the types of prompts children may encounter in high-stakes testing.

Scoring *Benchmark Assessment*

Questions 1–40 constitute a forty-point test. Multiple-choice items are worth one point each. The Writing Prompt (Test 2) should be scored using the rubric found below.

4-Point Scoring Rubric

	Focus	Organization	Support	Conventions
4	Writing maintains a consistent focus.	Writing employs an appropriate, consistent organizational strategy.	Writing is clearly supported by specific details. Word choice is precise and engaging.	Writing contains few, if any, errors.
3	Writing generally maintains a consistent focus.	Writing generally employs an organizational strategy.	Writing has supporting details. Word choice is correct but not precise.	Writing contains some errors.
2	Writing loses focus at times.	Writing attempts to use an organizational strategy.	Writing has few supporting details. Word choice is simple or unclear.	Writing contains several errors.
1	Writing does not have a consistent focus.	Writing has no organizational strategy.	Writing lacks supporting details. Word choice is limited.	Writing contains serious errors in the conventions of standard English.

Unscorable responses are unrelated to the topic, illegible, or contain little or no writing.

Evaluating *Benchmark Assessment* Scores

The goal of each benchmark assessment is to evaluate children's mastery of previously-taught material. The expectation is for children to score 80% or higher on the assessment as a whole. For children who would benefit from additional instruction, assign appropriate lessons from the Tier 2 online PDFs.

The Answer Keys in ***Benchmark Assessment*** provide the information you need to understand your children's performance and plan for their individualized instructional and intervention needs.

This column lists the instructional content that is assessed in each item.

Question	Answer	Content Focus	CCSS	Complexity

This column lists the CCSS alignment for each assessment item.

This column lists the Depth of Knowledge associated with each item.

22	A	Contractions with *not*	L.1.1	DOK 1
23	B	High-Frequency Words	RF.1.3g	DOK 1
24	C	Plot: Sequence	RL.1.3	DOK 2

Comprehension 4, 5, 6, 8, 9, 10, 11, 12, 15, 16, 17, 19, 20, 21, 24	/15	%
High-Frequency Words 1, 2, 7, 14, 23	/5	%
Structural Analysis 3, 13, 18, 22	/4	%

Scoring rows identify items by assessment focus and item type and allow for quick record keeping.

Read the poem "In the Park." Then answer Numbers 1 to 6.

In the Park

In a lake,
On a log,
I see a
Little frog.

GO ON →

In the grass
By the lake,
I see a
Big green snake.

In a hive,
On a tree,
I see a
Yellow bee.

Look up now,
In the sky,
Little birds
Flying by.

In the park,
I can see
Many things
Around me.

GO ON →

Name: ____________________ Date: ________

Now answer Numbers 1 to 6. Base your answers on the poem "In the Park."

1 You can see __________ things.

Ⓐ have

Ⓑ look

Ⓒ many

2 There is __________ dog in the park.

Ⓐ one

Ⓑ use

Ⓒ want

3 The little birds are __________ .

Ⓐ fly

Ⓑ flyed

Ⓒ flying

GO ON →

Name: ______________________ Date: __________

4 What word in the poem rhymes with <u>see</u>?

Ⓐ by

Ⓑ me

Ⓒ now

5 Which line repeats in the poem?

Ⓐ I see a

Ⓑ In a lake

Ⓒ Many things

6 What does the person in the poem see FIRST?

Ⓐ a snake

Ⓑ a frog

Ⓒ a bee

GO ON →

Read the story "A Banana Trip." Then answer Numbers 7 to 14.

A Banana Trip

Many people love bananas.
They are sweet and taste good.

Bananas grow in hot places.
These places are far away.
First, the workers pick the bananas.
The bananas go to a shed.
Workers wash the bananas.
Then they put them in boxes.

GO ON →

The bananas aren't yellow now.
They are green.
The bananas will get ripe later.

A truck takes them to a ship.
The ship goes over the sea.
Then it comes to land.
A truck picks up the bananas.
It takes the bananas to a store.

The bananas are yellow now.
Yum!
They are ready to eat!

GO ON →

From Plant to Shed

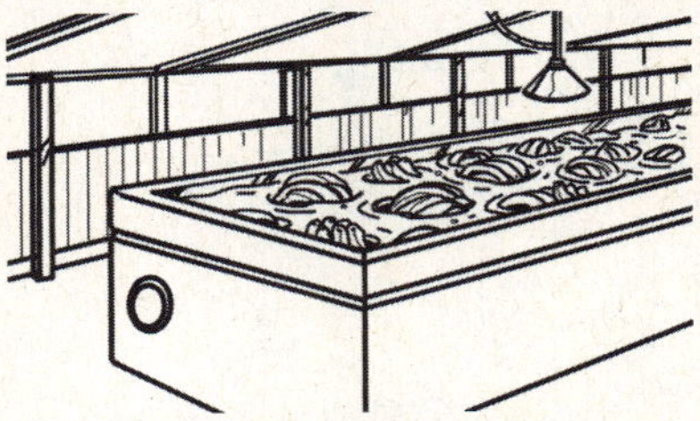

Washing in the Shed

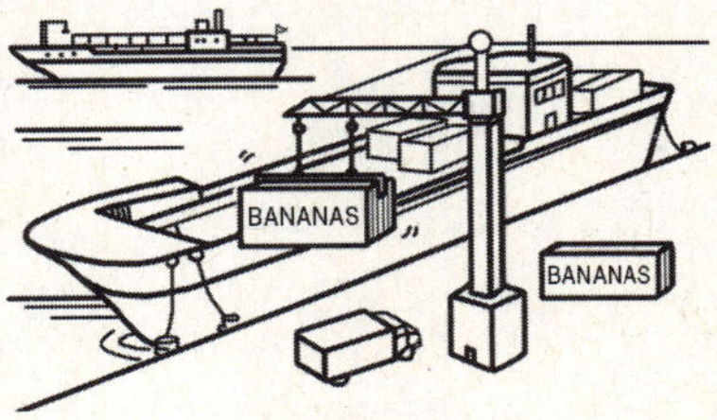

Across the Sea

Loading Up

Ready to Sell

GO ON →

Name: ______________________________ Date: ________

Now answer Numbers 7 to 14. Base your answers on the story "A Banana Trip."

7 Bananas are good to __________ .

Ⓐ eat

Ⓑ go

Ⓒ run

8 Where do bananas grow?

Ⓐ in hot places

Ⓑ in the store

Ⓒ in the sea

9 How are bananas at the store DIFFERENT from bananas picked from the tree?

Ⓐ Bananas at the store are green.

Ⓑ Bananas at the store are bigger.

Ⓒ Bananas at the store are yellow.

GO ON →

Name: ______________________________ Date: ________

10 What happens RIGHT AFTER the bananas are taken off the ship?

Ⓐ They go to the store.

Ⓑ The ship comes to land.

Ⓒ They are packed in boxes.

11 Look at the chart on page 7.
What happens to the bananas in the shed?

Ⓐ They are cut.

Ⓑ They get ripe.

Ⓒ They are washed.

12 The captions on page 7 tell you __________ .

Ⓐ how bananas get to the store

Ⓑ why bananas are yellow

Ⓒ how bananas get ripe

GO ON →

Name: ______________________________ Date: ________

13 Read this sentence from the story.

The bananas <u>aren't</u> yellow now.

Which words mean the same as <u>aren't</u>?

Ⓐ are not

Ⓑ have not

Ⓒ were not

14 At first, the bananas are __________ .

Ⓐ girl

Ⓑ green

Ⓒ grow

GO ON →

Read the story "Why Dogs Live with People." Then answer Numbers 15 to 24.

Why Dogs Live with People

Long ago, two dogs were cold.
They needed a place to stay.
One day, they went to Sage's house.
Sage the sheep said, "Come in.
You can stay here."

GO ON →

The dogs went inside.
But at night they barked.
The next morning, Sage was mad.
She said, "You must go!
You bark too much.
Lion will find my house.
Lion will eat me."

GO ON →

So the dogs left.
They went to Lance's house.
Lance the lion said, "Come in.
You can stay here."

GO ON →

The dogs went inside.
But at night they barked.
They barked all night.
The next morning, Lance said,
"Go away!
You bark too much.
People will find me.
They will put me in a zoo."

GO ON →

So the dogs found a family's house.
The family took them in.
They fed the dogs.
The dogs did not bark all night.
The dogs were happy.
The people were happy, too.
From that day on, dogs have lived with people.

GO ON →

Name: ______________________________ Date: __________

Now answer Numbers 15 to 24. Base your answers on the story "Why Dogs Live with People."

15 How many dogs are in the story?

Ⓐ 2 dogs

Ⓑ 3 dogs

Ⓒ 4 dogs

16 Why do the dogs look for a place to stay?

Ⓐ They are cold.

Ⓑ They are too hot.

Ⓒ They want to eat.

17 Where do the dogs go FIRST?

Ⓐ the lion's house

Ⓑ the family's house

Ⓒ the sheep's house

GO ON →

Name: ______________________________ Date: ________

18 The dogs were __________ .

Ⓐ barking

Ⓑ barked

Ⓒ barks

19 Sage says the lion will find her house because __________ .

Ⓐ she cannot sleep

Ⓑ the dogs bark too much

Ⓒ she wants more dogs to come to her house

20 Why does Lance the lion tell the dogs to go away?

Ⓐ They eat too much.

Ⓑ They bark too much.

Ⓒ They are too big for his house.

GO ON →

Name: ______________________ Date: __________

21 Where will people put Lance the lion if they find him?

Ⓐ in a house

Ⓑ on a ship

Ⓒ in a zoo

22 Read this sentence from the story.

The dogs <u>did not</u> bark all night.

Which word means the same as <u>did not</u>?

Ⓐ didn't

Ⓑ doesn't

Ⓒ don't

GO ON →

23 The people were __________, too.

Ⓐ after

Ⓑ happy

Ⓒ now

24 What happens LAST in the story?

Ⓐ The dogs go to the elephant's house.

Ⓑ The dogs go to the lion's house.

Ⓒ The dogs live with the family.

GO ON →

This is a story that Yoko wrote. Read the story. Then answer Numbers 25 to 29.

(1) My dog's name is fluffer. (2) I likes my dog. (3) I feed her (4) Mom and I giver her a bath. (5) Last week, I walks her every day. (6) Fluffer is a good pet.

GO ON →

Name: ______________________________ Date: ________

25 What is the BEST way to write sentence 1?

Ⓐ My Dog's name is fluffer.

Ⓑ My dog's name is Fluffer.

Ⓒ my dog's name is fluffer.

26 What is the BEST way to write sentence 2?

Ⓐ I like my dog.

Ⓑ I liked my dog.

Ⓒ I liking my dog.

27 What is the BEST way to write sentence 3?

Ⓐ I feed her?

Ⓑ I feed her,

Ⓒ I feed her.

GO ON →

Name: ______________________ Date: __________

28 What is the BEST way to write sentence 5?

Ⓐ Last week, I walk her every day.

Ⓑ Last week, I walked her every day.

Ⓒ Last week, I walking her every day.

29 What is sentence 6 about?

Ⓐ is

Ⓑ good

Ⓒ Fluffer

GO ON →

Read the story. Choose the word that correctly completes Numbers 30 to 34.

I ___(30)___ a new pet. ___(31)___ takes me to a pet store. We look at cats. We look at birds. I ___(32)___ a fish. My ___(33)___ name is Goldie. It ___(34)___ a good name!

GO ON →

Name: ______________________________ Date: ________

30 What answer should go in blank (30)?

Ⓐ want

Ⓑ wants

Ⓒ wanting

31 What answer should go in blank (31)?

Ⓐ dad

Ⓑ Dad

Ⓒ DAD

32 What answer should go in blank (32)?

Ⓐ gets

Ⓑ getting

Ⓒ will get

GO ON →

Name: ______________________________ Date: __________

33 What answer should go in blank (33)?

Ⓐ fish's

Ⓑ fishs

Ⓒ fish

34 What answer should go in blank (34)?

Ⓐ are

Ⓑ be

Ⓒ is

GO ON →

Name: ______________________ Date: ________

Choose the word that names the picture.

35 

Ⓐ bag
Ⓑ big
Ⓒ bug

36 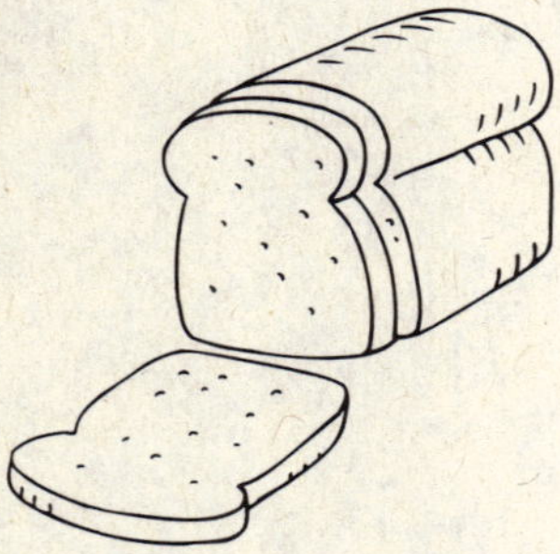

Ⓐ brad
Ⓑ bread
Ⓒ bride

37 

Ⓐ snag
Ⓑ drag
Ⓒ flag

GO ON →

Name: ______________________________ Date: __________

38 

Ⓐ ring
Ⓑ rank
Ⓒ rest

39 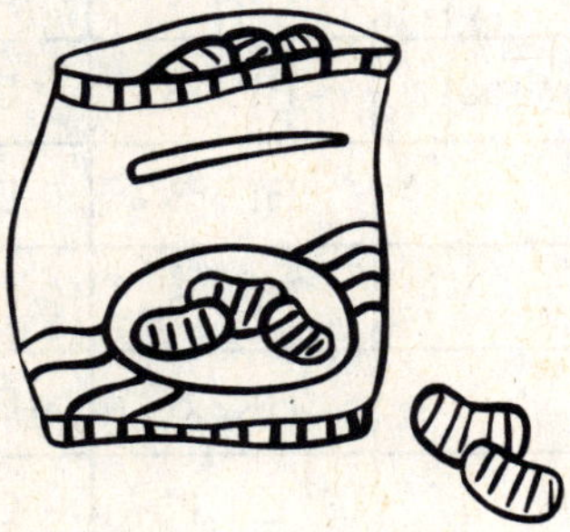

Ⓐ ship
Ⓑ chip
Ⓒ rich

40 

Ⓐ not
Ⓑ nut
Ⓒ note

STOP

Answer Key

Name: ______________________________

Question	Answer	Content Focus	CCSS	Complexity
1	C	High-Frequency Words	RF.1.3g	DOK 1
2	A	High-Frequency Words	RF.1.3g	DOK 1
3	C	Inflectional Ending *-ing*	RF.1.3f	DOK 2
4	B	Literary Element: Rhyme	RL.2.4	DOK 1
5	A	Literary Element: Repetition	RL.2.4	DOK 1
6	B	Plot: Sequence	RL.1.3	DOK 1
7	A	High-Frequency Words	RF.1.3g	DOK 1
8	A	Key Details	RI.1.1	DOK 1
9	C	Connections Within Text: Compare and Contrast	RI.1.3	DOK 2
10	A	Connections Within Text: Sequence	RI.1.3	DOK 2
11	C	Text Feature: Diagram	RI.1.6	DOK 1
12	A	Text Feature: Captions	RI.2.5	DOK 2
13	A	Contractions with *not*	L.1.1	DOK 1
14	B	High-Frequency Words	RF.1.3g	DOK 1
15	A	Key Details	RL.1.1	DOK 1
16	A	Plot: Cause and Effect	RL.1.3	DOK 2
17	C	Plot: Sequence	RL.1.3	DOK 1
18	A	Inflectional Ending *-ing*	RF.1.3f	DOK 2
19	B	Plot: Cause and Effect	RL.1.3	DOK 2
20	B	Plot: Cause and Effect	RL.1.3	DOK 2
21	C	Key Details	RL.1.1	DOK 1
22	A	Contractions with *not*	L.1.1	DOK 1
23	B	High-Frequency Words	RF.1.3g	DOK 1
24	C	Plot: Sequence	RL.1.3	DOK 2
25	B	Common and Proper Nouns	L.1.1b	DOK 1

Answer Key

Name: ______________________________

Question	Answer	Content Focus	CCSS	Complexity
26	A	Present-Tense Verbs	L.1.1e	DOK 1
27	C	Writing Sentences	L.1.2b	DOK 1
28	B	Past- and Future-Tense Verbs	L.1.1e	DOK 1
29	C	Nouns (as subject)	L.1.2c	DOK 1
30	A	Present-Tense Verbs	L.1.1e	DOK 1
31	B	Common and Proper Nouns	L.1.1b	DOK 1
32	C	Past- and Future-Tense Verbs	L.1.1e	DOK 1
33	A	Possessive Nouns	L.1.1b	DOK 1
34	C	Verbs (*is* and *are*)	L.1.1c	DOK 1
35	C	Short *u*	RF.1.3b	DOK 1
36	B	Short *e*: *e*, *ea*	RF.1.3b	DOK 1
37	C	Consonant Blends *r, l, s*	RF.1.3b	DOK 1
38	A	Consonant Digraphs *th, sh, -ng*	RF.1.3a	DOK 1
39	B	Consonant Digraphs *ch, -tch, wh, ph*	RF.1.3a	DOK 1
40	C	Long o: *o_e*	RF.1.3c	DOK 1

Comprehension 4, 5, 6, 8, 9, 10, 11, 12, 15, 16, 17, 19, 20, 21, 24	/15	%
High-Frequency Words 1, 2, 7, 14, 23	/5	%
Structural Analysis 3, 13, 18, 22	/4	%
English Language Conventions 25, 26, 27, 28, 29, 30, 31, 32, 33, 34	/10	%
Phonics 35, 36, 37, 38, 39, 40	/6	%
Total Benchmark Assessment Score	/40	%

Read the poem "At the Beach." Then answer Numbers 1 to 7.

At the Beach

by Janet Callahan

When I go to the beach on a summer day,
There's a special game I like to play.

With pails of sand, I build a wall.
I make it strong, I make it tall.

GO ON →

When waves wash in, they can't quite reach
The wall I've built upon the beach.

Then the waves get bigger, and before too long
They'll reach my wall, so tall and strong.

At last a great wave strikes my wall.
It leaves behind no wall at all.

So I run to the water and jump right in.
Now it's time to take a swim.

GO ON →

Name: ______________________________ Date: ________

Now answer Numbers 1 to 7. Base your answers on the poem "At the Beach."

1 Which word from the poem rhymes with beach?

Ⓐ great

Ⓑ reach

Ⓒ wash

2 Read this sentence.

There's a special game I like to play.

What does play mean in this sentence?

Ⓐ do something for fun

Ⓑ act a part in a show

Ⓒ make music

GO ON →

Name: ______________________________ Date: ________

3 The wall is made from __________ .

Ⓐ rocks

Ⓑ sand

Ⓒ shells

4 What word means the OPPOSITE of in?

Ⓐ out

Ⓑ quite

Ⓒ to

5 Which words from the poem show alliteration?

Ⓐ At last a great wave

Ⓑ When waves wash in

Ⓒ Then the waves get bigger

GO ON →

Name: ______________________________ Date: __________

6 What happens to the wall at the END of the poem?

Ⓐ The boy hops up and down on it.

Ⓑ A strong wind blows it over.

Ⓒ A big wave washes it away.

7 What is the LAST thing the speaker does in the poem?

Ⓐ gets a pail

Ⓑ builds a wall

Ⓒ jumps in the water

GO ON →

Read the story "Dad's Glasses." Then answer Numbers 8 to 13.

Dad's Glasses

Dad was walking around the house with a frown on his face. He needed his glasses so he could read the newspaper. Dad could not remember where he had put them.

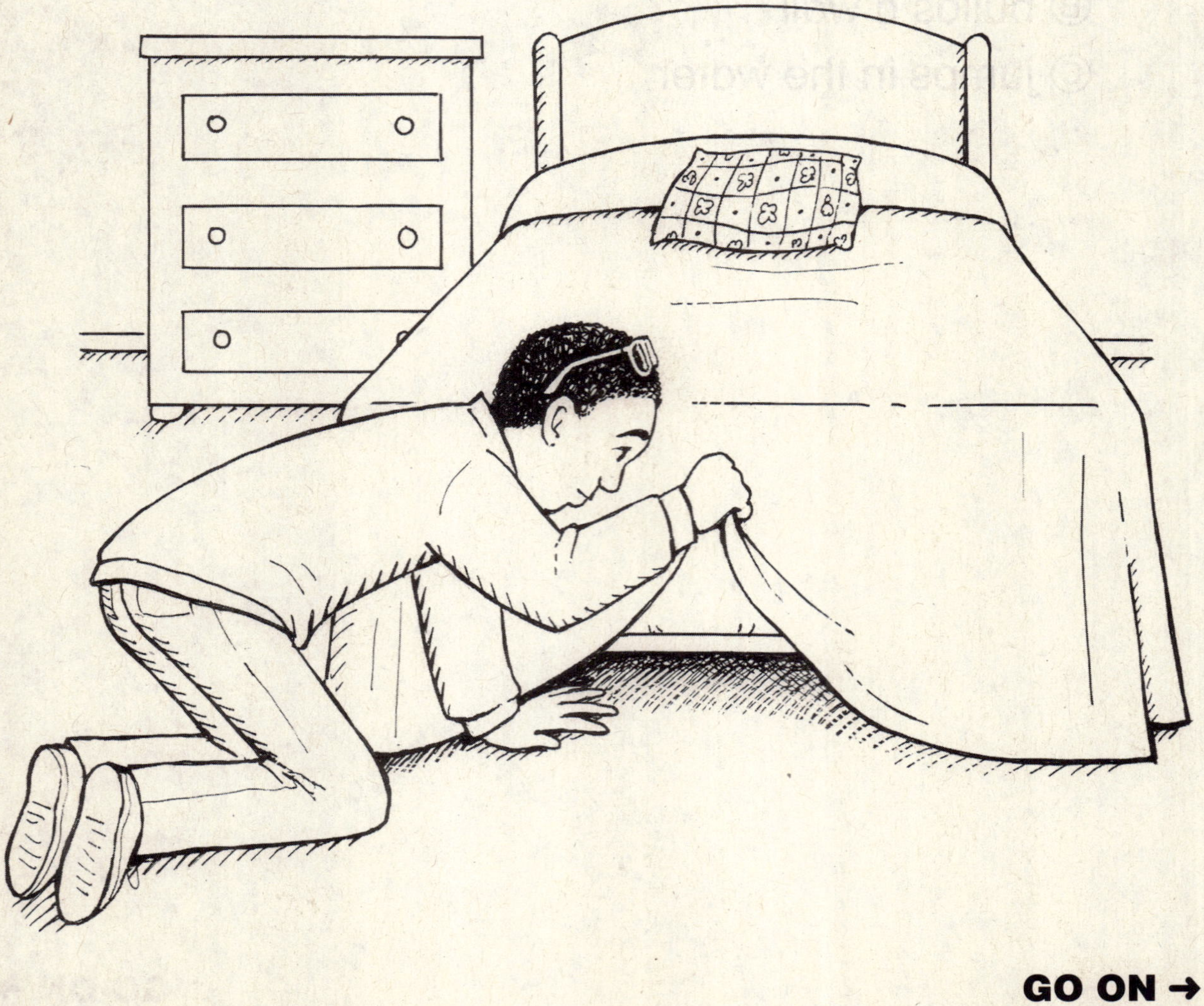

GO ON →

First, Dad looked in the bedroom. He looked on the bed table and under the bed.

Next, Dad opened the closet. He looked in the pockets of his brown coat. He looked in the pockets of his green jacket. He even looked inside his winter boots.

Then Dad went outside to the car. He looked on the seats of the car. He searched under the car seats, too.

Dad came back inside. He walked into the den and looked around. Then he sighed loudly.

GO ON →

Mom and Wendy were sitting in the den, and they heard Dad sigh.

"What's wrong?" asked Mom.

"I've looked everywhere for my glasses, but I can't find them," he said.

Wendy and Mom looked at Dad. Then they smiled at each other. Dad was always losing his glasses, but this time they were not lost. Mom and Wendy knew just where they were.

"Maybe Mom and I can help you," said Wendy.

"That would be great," said Dad. "I've looked in the bedroom, in the closet, and in the car. I don't know where else to look."

GO ON →

Now Mom and Wendy started to laugh.

Dad looked surprised. "What's so funny?" he asked.

"Look in the mirror and you'll find out," Mom answered.

When Dad looked in the mirror, he laughed, too. His glasses were on top of his head.

GO ON →

Name: ______________________________ Date: __________

Now answer Numbers 8 to 13. Base your answers on the story "Dad's Glasses."

8 How does Dad MOST LIKELY feel at the beginning of the story?

Ⓐ afraid

Ⓑ confused

Ⓒ happy

9 Dad is looking for his __________ .

Ⓐ boots

Ⓑ glasses

Ⓒ newspaper

10 Which word is a compound word?

Ⓐ inside

Ⓑ loudly

Ⓒ walked

GO ON →

Name: ______________________________ Date: ________

11 Read these sentences from the story.

He looked on the seats of the car. He <u>searched</u> under the car seats, too.

What does searched mean?

Ⓐ cleaned

Ⓑ looked

Ⓒ rested

12 Where are Dad's glasses?

Ⓐ under the bed

Ⓑ in the closet

Ⓒ on his head

13 What is the theme of this story?

Ⓐ We make silly mistakes sometimes.

Ⓑ We should never ask others for help.

Ⓒ When we make a mess, we should clean it up.

GO ON →

Read the story "A Wild Neighbor." Then answer Numbers 14 to 20.

A Wild Neighbor

Do you like to watch wild birds? If you do, you may have seen cardinals. Cardinals live in many different places. They can survive in all kinds of weather.

A male cardinal and a female cardinal look a lot alike. They are the same size and shape. Their faces are black. They have orange beaks. They have a special set of head feathers. It is called a crest. The crest looks like a party hat!

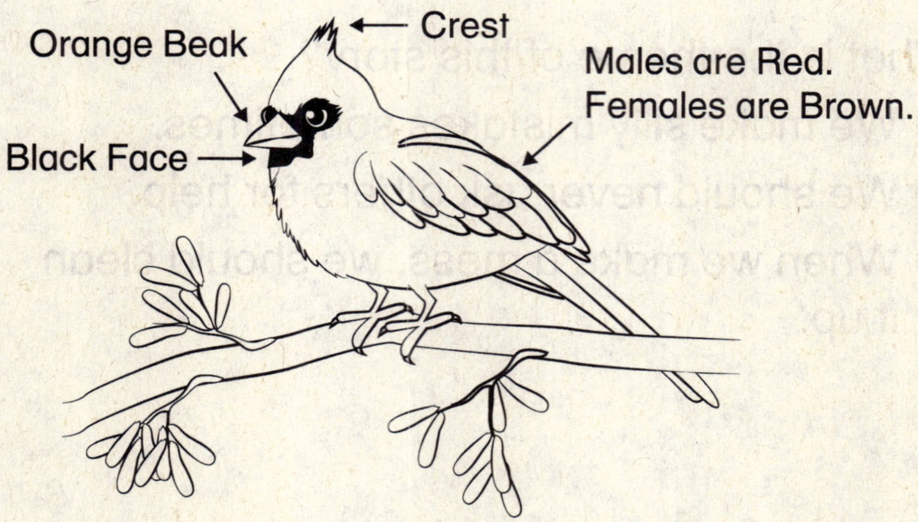

GO ON →

There is one big difference between males and females. It makes them easy to tell apart. The male's body is bright red. But the female is mostly brown. Her color makes her blend in with her nest. That's helpful when she stays in the nest to hatch her eggs.

Cardinals like to live close to the ground. They build their nests in bushes or short trees. They use twigs and bark to build a strong nest. But the nest must be soft on the inside. So the cardinals find bits of grass. They put the grass inside the nest. It makes a soft pad.

GO ON →

Do cardinals live near you? There is an easy way to find out. Put sunflower seeds in a bird feeder. Then have an adult hang the feeder outside your window. Cardinals love sunflower seeds. If they live nearby, they will find your feeder quickly! You can watch the cardinals as they eat.

Name: ______________________________ Date: ________

Now answer Numbers 14 to 20. Base your answers on the story "A Wild Neighbor."

14 "A Wild Neighbor" is about __________ .

Ⓐ birds in cages

Ⓑ birds called cardinals

Ⓒ many different kinds of birds

15 Why did the author write this story?

Ⓐ to give facts about cardinals

Ⓑ to tell a funny story about cardinals

Ⓒ to teach the reader how to build a nest for cardinals

16 Look at the diagram on page 12. Where is the cardinal's crest?

Ⓐ It is on its wings.

Ⓑ It is on its head.

Ⓒ It is on its tail.

GO ON →

Name: ______________________________ Date: ________

17 How is a female cardinal DIFFERENT from a male cardinal?

Ⓐ Her beak is orange, but his is black.

Ⓑ Her face is black, but his is brown.

Ⓒ Her body is brown, but his is red.

18 Why do cardinals put grass in their nests?

Ⓐ to make them strong

Ⓑ to make them green

Ⓒ to make them soft

GO ON →

Name: ______________________________ Date: __________

19 Cardinals love to eat __________ .

Ⓐ leaves and grass

Ⓑ sunflower seeds

Ⓒ bark and twigs

20 Read this sentence from the story.

If they live nearby, they will find your <u>feeder</u> quickly!

What is the root word of <u>feeder</u>?

Ⓐ er

Ⓑ fee

Ⓒ feed

GO ON →

Name: ______________________________ Date: ________

Choose the best answer.

21 Dad is __________ me a ride to school.

Ⓐ giving

Ⓑ giveing

Ⓒ givving

22 My teacher's name is __________ Parker.

Ⓐ Mr

Ⓑ Mr,

Ⓒ Mr.

GO ON →

Name: ______________________________ Date: __________

23 The __________ are singing.

Ⓐ childs

Ⓑ children

Ⓒ childrens

24 Please __________ your shoes before you take them off.

Ⓐ ties

Ⓑ retie

Ⓒ untie

GO ON →

Read the story. Choose the word that correctly completes Numbers 25 to 29.

I ___(25)___ a brother. ___(26)___ name is Nick. Nick is two years ___(27)___ than I am. I like Nick ___(28)___ he is always kind. He shares ___(29)___ with me. What a great brother he is!

GO ON →

Name: ______________________________ Date: __________

25 Which answer should go in blank (25)?

Ⓐ has

Ⓑ have

Ⓒ having

26 Which answer should go in blank (26)?

Ⓐ He

Ⓑ Him

Ⓒ His

27 Which answer should go in blank (27)?

Ⓐ old

Ⓑ older

Ⓒ oldest

GO ON →

Name: ______________________ Date: ________

28 Which answer should go in blank (28)?

Ⓐ because

Ⓑ but

Ⓒ or

29 Which answer should go in blank (29)?

Ⓐ everywhere

Ⓑ everything

Ⓒ everyone

GO ON →

This is a story that Maya wrote. Read the story. Then answer Numbers 30 to 34.

(1) My grandfather has a orange tree. (2) Yesterday, I pick some oranges. (3) Then grandpa made orange juice. (4) He gave me a glass, and I tasted it. (5) That juice was so sweet (6) I'm glad I picked them oranges.

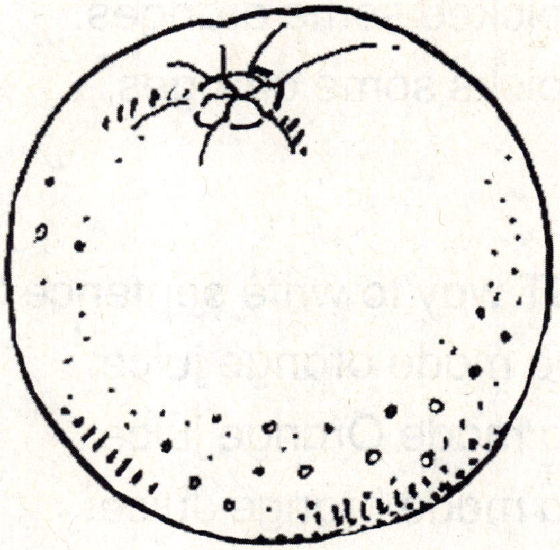

GO ON →

Name: ______________________________ Date: ________

30 What is the BEST way to write sentence 1?

Ⓐ My grandfather has an orange tree.

Ⓑ My grandfather has some orange tree.

Ⓒ My grandfather has these orange tree.

31 What is the BEST way to write sentence 2?

Ⓐ Yesterday, I picking some oranges.

Ⓑ Yesterday, I picked some oranges.

Ⓒ Yesterday, I picks some oranges.

32 What is the BEST way to write sentence 3?

Ⓐ Then Grandpa made orange juice.

Ⓑ Then grandpa made Orange juice.

Ⓒ Then grandpa made orange Juice.

GO ON →

Name: ______________________ Date: ________

33 What is the BEST way to write sentence 5?

Ⓐ That juice was so sweet?

Ⓑ That juice was so sweet!

Ⓒ That juice was so sweet,

34 What is the BEST way to write sentence 6?

Ⓐ I'm glad I picked this oranges.

Ⓑ I'm glad I picked that oranges.

Ⓒ I'm glad I picked those oranges.

GO ON →

Name: ______________________ Date: ________

Choose the word that names the picture.

35

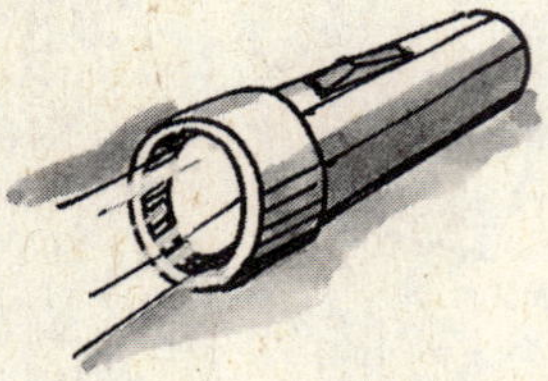

Ⓐ let
Ⓑ late
Ⓒ light

36

Ⓐ pool
Ⓑ pail
Ⓒ pile

37

Ⓐ pay
Ⓑ paint
Ⓒ point

GO ON →

Name: ______________________ Date: ________

38

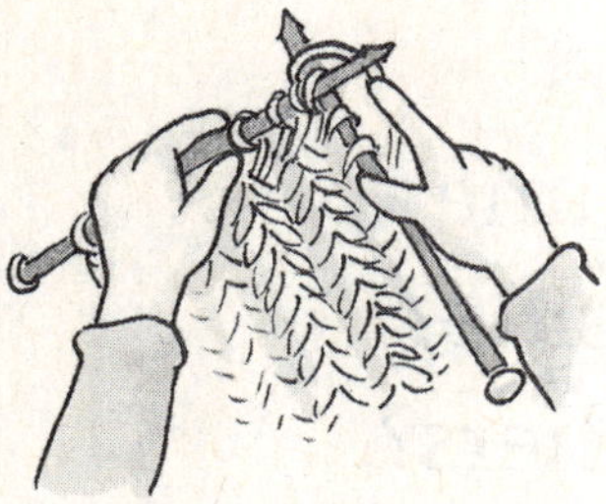

Ⓐ kit

Ⓑ knit

Ⓒ night

39

Ⓐ three

Ⓑ tread

Ⓒ thread

40

Ⓐ bar

Ⓑ bear

Ⓒ bore

STOP

Writing Prompt

What do you think is the best game to play? Do you play it at home or outside? Do you play it by yourself or with others?

Write a paragraph that gives your opinion about the best game to play. Make sure to tell what the best game is and why you think so.

Use the space below to plan your writing. Write your paragraph on the lines on page 29.

Name: ____________________ Date: ________

Final Draft

Answer Key

Name: ____________________

Question	Answer	Content Focus	CCSS	Complexity
1	B	Literary Element: Rhyme	RL.2.4	DOK 1
2	A	Context Clues: Multiple Meanings	L.K.4a	DOK 1
3	B	Key Details	RL.1.1	DOK 1
4	A	Antonyms	L.4.5c	DOK 1
5	B	Literary Element: Alliteration	RL.2.4	DOK 1
6	C	Plot: Cause and Effect	RL.1.3	DOK 2
7	C	Plot: Sequence	RL.1.3	DOK 1
8	B	Point of View	RL.2.6	DOK 2
9	B	Key Details	RL.1.1	DOK 1
10	A	Compound Words	L.2.4d	DOK 1
11	B	Context Clues: Sentence Clues	L.1.4a	DOK 2
12	C	Plot: Problem and Solution	RL.1.3	DOK 2
13	A	Theme	RL.1.2	DOK 3
14	B	Main Topic and Key Details	RI.1.2	DOK 2
15	A	Author's Purpose	RI.2.6	DOK 2
16	B	Text Features: Diagram	RI.1.6	DOK 1
17	C	Connections Within Text: Compare and Contrast	RI.1.3	DOK 2
18	C	Connections Within Text: Problem and Solution	RI.1.3	DOK 2
19	B	Key Details	RI.1.1	DOK 1
20	C	Root Words	L.1.4c	DOK 1
21	A	Inflectional Endings *-ed, -ing*	RF.1.3f	DOK 2
22	C	Abbreviations	L.1.2	DOK 1
23	B	Plurals (irregular)	L.1.1c	DOK 1
24	C	Prefixes *re-*, *un-*, *pre-*	L.1.4b	DOK 1
25	B	Verbs: *Was/Were, Go/Do, Has/Have, See/Saw*	L.1.1e	DOK 1

Answer Key

Name: ______________________________

Question	Answer	Content Focus	CCSS	Complexity
26	C	Possessive Pronouns	L.1.1d	DOK 1
27	B	Adjectives That Compare: *-er* and *-est*	L.1.1f	DOK 1
28	A	Conjunctions	L.1.1g	DOK 1
29	B	Indefinite Pronouns	L.1.1d	DOK 1
30	A	Other Adjectives	L.1.1h	DOK 1
31	B	Past- and Future-Tense Verbs	L.1.1e	DOK 1
32	A	Common and Proper Nouns	L.1.1b	DOK 1
33	B	End Punctuation	L.1.2b	DOK 1
34	C	Other Adjectives	L.1.1h	DOK 1
35	C	Long i: *i, i_e, y, igh, ie*	RF.1.3c	DOK 1
36	A	Variant Vowel Digraphs /ü/: *oo (tool), u, u_e, ew, ue, ui, ou*	RF.1.3c	DOK 1
37	C	Diphthongs *ou, ow, oi, oy*	RF.1.3	DOK 1
38	B	Silent Letters *wr, kn, gn*	RF.1.3	DOK 1
39	C	Three-Letter Blends *scr, spl, spr, str, thr, shr*	RF.1.3	DOK 1
40	B	*r*-Controlled Vowels *ar, er, ir, oar, or, ore, ur, air, are, ear*	RF.1.3	DOK 1
Writing Prompt	See below	Opinion	W.1.1, L.1.1, L.1.2	DOK 3

Comprehension 1, 3, 5, 6, 7, 8, 9, 12, 13, 14, 15, 16, 17, 18, 19	/15	%
Vocabulary Strategies 2, 4, 10, 11, 20	/5	%
Structural Analysis 21, 22, 23, 24	/4	%
English Language Conventions 25, 26, 27, 28, 29, 30, 31, 32, 33, 34	/10	%
Phonics 35, 36, 37, 38, 39, 40	/6	%
Total Benchmark Assessment Score	/40	%

Writing Prompt

Refer to the scoring criteria in the Teacher Introduction.